It's Time to Align

The Most Powerful Self-Help Book Ever Written

Allen Lottinger

BALBOA.
PRESS

A DIVISION OF HAY HOUSE

Balboa Press books may be ordered through booksellers or by contacting:

Balboa Press
A Division of Hay House
1663 Liberty Drive
Bloomington, IN 47403
www.balboapress.com
1 (877) 407-4847

Because of the dynamic nature of the Internet, any web addresses or links contained in this book may have changed since publication and may no longer be valid. The views expressed in this work are solely those of the author and do not necessarily reflect the views of the publisher, and the publisher hereby disclaims any responsibility for them.

The author of this book does not dispense medical advice or prescribe the use of any technique as a form of treatment for physical, emotional, or medical problems without the advice of a physician, either directly or indirectly. The intent of the author is only to offer information of a general nature to help you in your quest for emotional and spiritual well-being. In the event you use any of the information in this book for yourself, which is your constitutional right, the author and the publisher assume no responsibility for your actions.

Any people depicted in stock imagery provided by Thinkstock are models, and such images are being used for illustrative purposes only. Certain stock imagery © Thinkstock.

Printed in the United States of America.

ISBN: 978-1-4525-2152-7 (sc)
ISBN: 978-1-4525-2154-1 (hc)
ISBN: 978-1-4525-2153-4 (e)

Library of Congress Control Number: 2014915758

Balboa Press rev. date: 10/13/2014

Contents

"To trust in God means to trust in the universal laws."

The Author

Introduction

In this book we will discuss the term vibration and its relationship to our experienced reality. It is important to define before we begin exactly what vibration is. To understand this we need to realize that everything in the physical world is at its base pure energy and that energy is vibrating at a certain speed.

Most of the natural world, excluding humans, is vibrating at a constant state. Humans, and other conscious beings, are unique in that we have the ability to raise or lower our vibration based on our choices. High vibrational choices will align us with things that resonate at a similar frequency. Low vibrational choices will do the same.

What happens when we raise our vibration? Wealth, love, peace, purpose. Our seven chakras start moving again. Everything of a different vibration falls away. The dark forces that are attempting to suppress the vibration of our planet cannot work in that environment but other more benevolent entities can. We become aligned with our vortex of creation (our crown chakra) and high vibrational energy, which attracts desirable things, is allowed to flow into our reality.

Vibration is important because it determines the degree to which our desires become a reality. I mentioned the vortex of creation. This term comes from the teachings of Esther Hicks and is used to describe the creative power we all have. Another term some use is the higher self or the crown chakra but for our purposes let's stick with the vortex of creation.

As we discuss the importance of raising our vibration, this is related to the vortex of creation. What is a vortex? It is a spinning "tornado," just to keep it simple. We each have one located right above our head. What does a tornado do? It sucks things from one place to another. In the case of our vortex of creation, it is literally sucking high vibrational energy into our lives. This energy attracts things and experiences that resonate with it, usually along the lines of health, love, peace and prosperity.

Why is this important for us to know? Because our vibration controls the speed at which our vortex is spinning and therefore bringing that energy into our lives. If we can manage to focus on a few areas that will raise our personal vibration, the universe will have no choice but to respond flooding us with pure high vibration energy that will affect all areas of our lives. By raising our personal vibration we are opening the spicket that will allow the universe to work in this way.

If we close the spicket or let it remain closed, the complete opposite is true. We will be deprived of all that we desire and will not accomplish what we were put on this earth to do. We were put here to be conscious creators and to make this world a better place by bringing this high vibrational energy into our planet. Whatever comes after that as far as specific manifestations is up to us but as long as we are bringing in the high vibrational energy and putting that energy to work, we can't go wrong.

When our vibration is low, the spicket is closed or dripping. Our vortex becomes stagnant and our creative powers become greatly reduced if not stopped. This is the norm and leads to unfulfilling lives. We are cut off from the creative energy of the universe and left to fend for ourselves whereas if our vibration is high, our vortex is moving and gaining momentum. All those things we are trying to attract into our lives through our desires, thoughts and feelings begin to flow effortlessly. As we are filled with this energy, our chakras (vortexes) become engaged and start spinning faster. Any low vibrational energy we have accumulated is flushed out to make room for high vibrational energy. Just like our digestive system keeps what is good and gets rid of the junk, our energy body does the same by taking in high vibrational energy and releasing any low vibrational energy. This is an endless process because there are always new and higher vibrational energies for us to consume as we are able to handle it.

This is why the work of raising our vibration is so important. A high vibration will allow this energy to flow into our lives and manifest powerfully while low vibration will block it allowing no manifestation and the likelihood we will be manipulated by others. I would suggest we live in the time when this vibration is being purposely suppressed for reasons we will discuss. I would even go so far as to say that most of us have a vortex of creation that is completely stagnant and therefore we are left floundering around not really accomplishing what we were put on this planet to do - to become conscious creators.

Vibration is the key to engaging our vortex and getting it moving like it should be. In this book we will focus on what I believe to be the key actions which can significantly lower or raise our vibration. Focusing on these areas will empower us to take charge of our lives for the better.

Once we follow these guidelines to raise our vibration, it is the law of the universe that we will align with our vortex and allow it to become engaged. The whole process is one of ease. Our only role is to do the things that will raise our vibration while avoiding the things that lower it. After that the natural flow of the universe will take over. There is really no additional effort on our part. We can sit back and enjoy the lives we were meant to have all along but were suppressed by our own choices.

While many books talk about the law of attraction and even the vortex of creation, most are overlooking a very simple truth. There are forces conspiring to keep us from accessing these higher energies by keeping us vibrating at a very low frequency. Once we learn the ways in which our vibration is being suppressed and the things we can do to raise it, attracting good things and engaging our vortex (two terms meaning the same thing) will happen effortlessly. Suddenly Yoda's admonition "there is no try" begins to make sense.

Law of attraction books seem to be lacking in an understanding of the mechanics of the universe. The idea that we need to be constantly thinking good thoughts is certainly a nice goal, however, the reality is that this can be exhausting and impotent if we don't have an underlying foundation on which to build. That foundation is our frequency of vibration and a vortex that is flowing.

There are simple things we can do which will greatly increase our vibration, which I will lay out in this book. Once these steps are in place our vibration begins to rise naturally and at that point our vortex begins moving, sucking in high vibrational energy. This is what people mean when they talk about the law of attraction and attracting good things into our life. The process of creation consists of three simple steps, according to Esther Hicks. The following is how she lays it out in *The Vortex:*

1. *Ask. (And the contrast of life experience causes you to do that.)*
2. *Answer. (That is not the work of you from your physical perspective, but, instead, the work of Non-Physical Source Energy.)*
3. *Allow. (You must find a way to be a Vibrational Match to what you are asking for or you will not allow it into your experience even though the answer is available for you.)*

The fact is that most people already know what they want in life but if we aren't vibrating and therefore resonating with the creative energy of the universe, we have little chance of attracting specific manifestations. Unlimited free high vibrational energy, which is the key to being a conscious creator, can only come into our lives if we are resonating with it. Once our vibration has been raised sufficiently, this universal energy will have no choice but to flow into our lives. Alignment with our vision of the ideal life will take place automatically as this high vibrational energy goes to work in our experiences.

For example, my desire is health, love, peace and prosperity. Reading some law of attraction books would leave me with the impression I need to constantly think about these things for them to come into my life. There is a certain amount of truth in this because we do need to resonate with the creative energy of the universe for it to flow into our lives and attract these things. However, just thinking and feeling the things we desire to create will not get us there unless our vibration is sufficiently raised.

It is better to first take the steps to raise our vibration at which point the creative energy of the universe can flow into our lives effortlessly. That is when we will really begin attracting. Once on this path the sky is the limit and each day we can grow more and more in alignment with these vibrations. We can always increase our vibration and as we do our vortex of creation will respond by spinning faster and faster, sucking in more and higher vibrations from the universe. The result will be quicker and more focused manifestation of our desires. This is the law of attraction at work.

Living a low vibrational existence takes a lot of effort where as a high vibrational existence is filled with ease. A good analogy of the effort required to maintain a low vibrational existence is like trying to hold a beach ball under water. We are fighting against the natural order of things. Living a high vibrational existence aligned with the universe is like letting the beach ball go and allowing it to rise to the surface. Life becomes easy. All the energy previously used to maintain a low vibration is freed up.

At that point our vibration and the universe will begin to feed on one another. As our vibration rises, our vortex will spin faster which in turn will cause our vibration to rise some more. It is an endless process we could call many things: evolution, enlightenment, or ascension. This path is such a joy that there is not much danger of turning back once we experience the full power of our creative energies in action. That would be like choosing death over life.

Once our vibration is raised and our vortex is flowing our lives become an adventure of creative possibilities before thought unattainable. As we break free from the low vibrational prison others around us will see that it is possible and will follow our lead. It is in this way that the world will change for the better.

At its core, vibration is energy in motion or emotion. Low vibrational feelings are always net negative and high vibrational feelings are always net positive. On the quantum physics level this is expressed as literally the speed at which the energy which makes up our bodies and thoughts is vibrating.

Trying to figure out what activities are low vibrational versus which ones are high vibrational can be exhausting. In a complex universe there are always grey areas which could endlessly be debated (low vibration activity). The ten areas of focus I lay out in this book seem to be powerful steps to raising our vibration. Small details and nuances would do nothing more than distract our attention from the main goal, which is to quickly and massively raise our vibrations and get our vortexes moving. To get the most bang for our buck if you will.

Once this is accomplished, the scales will fall from our eyes and we will have the ability to fine tune our vibration to ever higher levels. We will gain greater insight into what actions truly help us to maintain a healthy flowing vortex of creation and which actions cause it to decrease in momentum. Once we experience our high vibration in conjunction with a flowing vortex, which we will call alignment, the work of raising our vibration to higher levels is no longer exhausting but something we will enjoy doing as co-creators in this vast universe of ours.

It will be like finally learning to swim after sitting around for eons at the bottom of the pool in a comatose state. We are the beach ball that has been suppressed under the water all these years and is ready to be set free and rise to the surface. This is literally a metaphysical reality that, once put into practice, cannot be denied.

And this is not simply a self-help fad that is designed to sell books and then ultimately leave the reader discontented and more skeptical. Our planet is in dire need of people to raise their vibrations which are being suppressed purposely by dark forces that feed off of low vibrational energy. These forces are desperate to cut us off from the high vibrational energy of the universe. Though it has been endlessly abused, we could use the word "god" to describe this universal energy.

This is a controversial but important point that we really need to come to terms with if we are to have any chance of raising our vibrations. It does no good to ignore the elephant in the room which is that there is a reason our vibrations are being suppressed and we are therefore being denied access to our full creative abilities. Denial will do us no good in this area. The truth will set us free.

So what are these forces that have it out for us? For simplicity sake let's call them archons. This is a term used by Gnostics to identify non-human inter-dimensionals akin to what some would describe as demons, jinn or reptile-like creatures. This doesn't mean that is what they are, they are just terms used by people for centuries to describe these forces.

It probably isn't helpful for our purposes to get too specific in trying to identify the dark forces suppressing human vibration as it could become a distraction and stir up religiously motivated emotions. Our focus, rather, should be simply to understand what these forces are up to and to protect ourselves from their influence.

However, just for reference sake, we should at least understand that humans have been dealing with these "spiritual" beings for thousands of years. The group I mentioned called Gnostics were early philosophers who believed that knowledge is the way to salvation of the soul from the material world. They saw the material world as created through an intermediary being (the demiurge), who was imperfect or even evil, rather than directly by "god."

In late antiquity the term archon was used by Gnostics to refer to several servants of the demiurge, the "creator god" that stood between the human race and a transcendent god that could only be reached through knowledge (truth vibrations). In this context they have the role of the angels and demons of the Old Testament.

It is important to note that humans only see a very small percentage of our surroundings. We see the portion known as visible light. But what else is there? Well, we know that there are radio waves, Wi-Fi signals, etc. all around us. So it shouldn't be too difficult to acknowledge the reality that we just don't see all there is metaphysically.

At this point we could get bogged down into how the mind works and how it sees what it wants to or is programmed to see but honestly this discussion is way above my pay grade. So let's keep it simple, there are things we don't perceive - just like our vortex of creation. Whether we acknowledge it or not, it is there and is affecting our lives.

So what are the archons really? Well we don't know for sure but evidence is everywhere – from worldwide religious and mythological accounts commonly describing ancient encounters with advanced beings to anomalous archaeological sites like the pyramids indicating past use of superior technology.

Some believe that mankind is being enslaved by forces who are technologically and psychically advanced. Their ultimate goal, they say, is to assimilate us into their empire and parasitically exploit us for our biological, energetic, and physical resources. To accomplish this, our connection with the universe (our vibration and vortex) needs to be shut down otherwise the jig is up. These are low vibrational entities and therefore they would not be able to operate in an environment with which they do not resonate. For the purposes of this book I will focus on the energetic exploitation and how putting an end to that will take care of the other two areas. Raising our vibration is really the key to ending this manipulation.

Though I don't want to get too lost in the *Star Wars* universe let's at least take a quick look at what some believe is the big picture going on in our galaxy. The following comes from an article called *Synopsis of the Alien Master Plan* on Davidicke. com and is an interesting theory of the mechanics of the manipulation taking place in our world. While none of this information can be quantified, it none the less provides a framework from which we can begin to discuss how to overcome the obstacles to our alignment that are definitely present, wherever they came from:

"Given their technological superiority, why don't hostile alien forces just take over the planet? For strategic reasons, their invasion is a drawn out process rather than a single spectacular blitzkrieg as one might expect, though the latter can be used to finalize the invasion once the first phase has spiritually tranquilized the target population. There are many problems with an overt invasion using physical force. History has shown that visible tyrants are also visible targets who quickly fall if they reveal themselves before total control has been established. Smarter tyrants stay hidden and cleverly manipulate the population into first defeating and enslaving itself.

Cosmic tyrants exist who seek to assimilate entire worlds into their empire. The premature invasion of those who have targeted us could lead to conflicts threatening the two resources they have come here to exploit: earth and its inhabitants. They prefer that we willingly hand over ourselves and the planet with the least amount of resistance. This can only happen under the condition that we are unaware of their true nature or agenda. Preparing such deception requires much groundwork. Thus, they have chosen to covertly and patiently manipulate human society toward that end.

Their preferred method of subversion is to create elite among the population who do the dirty work of enslaving the rest. What we know as the "secret government" is an occult technocracy comprised of these elite humans. The secret government is using problem-reaction-solution techniques to frame world conflicts as pretexts for the establishment of a 'New World Order,' an overt global totalitarian regime that will lockdown any potential for resistance and secure earth for easy assimilation into the alien empire.

Why have they not finished their invasion sooner, back when our technology was too primitive to damage their desired resources?

As mentioned, they prefer we willingly hand over our collective freewill. Only recently have we become technologically and politically advanced enough to create and support the infrastructure of the New World Order through which we are intended to enslave ourselves. They make their victims dig their own graves."

We don't really have to accept this or not for us to benefit from raising our vibration and engaging our vortex. That process is a law of the universe and will work no matter what we believe. However, understanding that our vibration is being purposely suppressed can serve as a catalyst for us to overcome the manipulation. We are truly the frog in warm water and the heat is slowly being turned up on us. The time is now to take control of the situation while we still can.

Where did these entities that showed up so many centuries ago come from? We don't really know but suffice it to say that we live in a huge galaxy. What is the figure? Half a trillion star systems? And then another half trillion additional galaxies? And this is just what we know from our limited knowledge. So I think on the point of exactly where they came from we should just concede ignorance for the time being and be at peace with that. We should be more concerned with what they represent - a very low vibrational energy that threatens to destroy this planet and the quality of life of its inhabitants.

I'm sure at some point in our evolution when we are on the road to peace and harmony some researchers will have great insights into who the manipulators were - demons from hell or lizards from Draco. Not much difference in my book but the priority for now is to get rid of the fuckers. The only way to do that is to raise our vibration individually and then collectively so these entities will have to leave. Then we can discuss who they were. If the human race can raise our vibration they will have no choice but to hightail it back whence they came. Our planet would be flooded with pure high vibrational energy from the universe. The manipulators would be like fish out of water, not able to function in that environment.

Again, we are at our base pure energy. All energy is vibrating. Archons feed on a low vibrational energy so to escape the matrix they have created we should make raising our vibration our highest priority. Everything of a low vibration will disappear when we do this. Guilt, repression, hatred, violence, and fear are all delicacies to the archons. To counter this we, as expressions of infinite consciousness, should vibrate with love, peace, understanding, the natural world and silence, things they cannot palate.

The ten areas we will discuss are good ways to begin focusing on these higher vibrational energies. Once aligned with these energies all the lower vibrational entities will fall away. It is a law of the universe that the two cannot coexist. As our vibrations raise all lower (less powerful) vibrations must flee. And as our vortex begins spinning and gains momentum, our vibration will raise even more and on and on. That is really the "secret" that law of attraction promoters should be talking about.

This is why we live in such an important time period. We are deciding the type of world we will leave not just to our children but to countless future generations. Will it be a place where people are controlled by fear? Where guilt and repression cripple our souls? And where violence and a cycle of death are commonplace? Or will it be a world where we learn to commune with the universe through regular periods of silence as communities and raise our collective vibration to one of love, peace and harmony. Then the answers to many of our most pressing problems will flow from the universe, but not until we quiet our minds collectively and refuse to be manipulated by forces which do not have our best interest in mind.

Of course, the choice is ours and we can certainly choose to live in the world the archons are working to create, *The Hunger Games* society if you will. Free will is one of the laws of the universe and if humans can come to accept violence, fear, and suffering as normal aspects of this world then we certainly have that right. We will not be judged by anything except that which we freely choose. Over time we become desensitized to the realities of our choices and can literally create our own hell - cut off from the highest energy this universe has to offer. Once the low vibrational soup of our own creation becomes normal to us, our progeny will not know anything different and will become almost completely severed from the infinite consciousness of the universe. Once this happens we would degenerate into little more than cyborgs with very little creative force. We can see the early stages of this going on today with young people locked into their computer devices. We can become more and more like the low vibrational archons who are methodically working to manipulate us into that future which is each day becoming more and more alarmingly a reality.

But there is another way and that is the purpose of this book. We will focus in on ten key areas of our lives that determine our individual vibration in a major way. We can raise our vibration and end all the manipulation in very short order, it is simply up to us to make the decision to do so. So let us begin.

One quick note, as we begin this journey it is important to be aware of the forces working against us. When the archons created bloodlines thousands of years ago to facilitate their political, spiritual and economic control of the planet, they did not take a break. The process of control, which I like to call the hive mind, is well advanced and infiltrates every aspect of our lives, including family and relationships. Be mindful that as we attempt to raise our vibration, archontic forces will be working methodically to discourage us from attaining this alignment. They do not want us to reconnect with the universe. Don't worry about this though because a high vibrational existence is infinitely more powerful than the low vibration of the archons. As long as we keep focused on raising our individual vibrations, everything not resonating with us will fall away.

Also remember that as we raise our vibration and get our vortexes moving again, the collective vibration of our planet will be affected in ways we may never know. This is the true benefit of our quest because the entire universe will open to us as we make the choice of alignment. And that's when it will get really interesting.

The purpose of this list of suggestions is not to let the perfect be the enemy of the good. I'm sure there are many additional dietary and other considerations that can impact our vibration. What I wanted to do was to focus in on the areas, as I stated before, that will powerfully raise our vibrations so much so that after a couple of months or so of putting these steps into action we will be freed from the slavery of this low vibrational matrix and begin transforming the world one person at a time.

A. Things That Lower Vibration

1

Masturbation/ Prostitution

So why begin with masturbation and prostitution? Because these topics, though taboo, are huge factors in our vibration. So much energy is either lost or gained during sexual acts that they really are key to understanding how to raise our vibration. We should be aware of what is going on vibrationally when we have different sexual experiences. Then at least we will become "educated consumers" of sex.

The common denominator between masturbation and prostitution is that we are not benefiting energetically from a free-willed consensual sexual act, which we will get into shortly. Sex has the ability to raise our vibration more than perhaps any other act with the possible exception of meditation. Once we realize what is going on energetically during different sex acts we will at least have the information to make informed decisions.

To keep it simple high vibrational sex produces energy and raises our vibration while low vibrational sex drains our energy. Distinguishing between the two will of course be controversial but let's give it a shot. It is worth it to tackle this issue off the bat because most of what we think about, guys anyway, is sexual and nothing else will matter unless we get the sex issue settled.

The good news is that to raise our vibration we don't need to give up any sex, as we will see in later chapters. We only need to focus on the most energetically and physically satisfying forms of it. It should not be a tough sell but I know that any sexual topic will automatically provoke resistance. Believe me, I am not one to write a catechism. People have the right and freedom to enjoy their sexuality, but we need to be honest as well. If we truly have a desire to raise our vibrations and end the control system put in place by the archons, we need to fully understand what holds us back.

The topic of masturbation is a touchy one because nine out of ten people do it and the tenth person is probably lying about it. Though people will argue about it endlessly, I think most of us know instinctively that masturbation is a huge factor when it comes to our energy bodies. I know it is tough to hear but stopping the practice is key to raising our vibration.

Just put aside for a moment the energy lost in the practice, which is substantial, and consider the effects of habit and isolation that result. Masturbation does not require a partner and is extremely pleasurable which means it is easy to overindulge. The practice is nearly impossible to stop once the habit has been developed. Think of the *Seinfeld* episode with "the contest," how stressed out they all became when trying to give up masturbation for just a few days. Most of us are really wired into the habit of masturbation which, though difficult to escape, is not impossible.

If you decide to stop reading here please feel free to do so. For some the thought of not masturbating may in fact be a deal breaker. For others it may stir up emotions associated with being told by a religious authority that they could go to hell for doing it or some other silly fable. Either way it is a tough sell and I am not naive enough to think otherwise. However, if we truly desire to raise our vibration then nothing is impossible.

In the end the benefits of giving up this practice greatly outweigh the struggle. For starters, energy and creativity greatly increase when we become "masters of our domain."

Self-control also increases as well as mental clarity. All these things are nice, but the real net positive when we stop masturbating is that our vibration is raised which allows us to have an alignment with the high vibrational energy of the universe. This creates a domino effect of getting our vortex moving and helping to release us from the matrix of the archons. When our vortex kicks into gear we will become so interested in our creative abilities and high vibrational sex that we frankly won't have the time nor the desire to masturbate. These benefits may well be the catalyst we need to let go of the highly addictive habit of masturbation which unfortunately is a valuable asset to the archons.

In addition to all the metaphysical reasons to forego masturbation, there are a ton of health reasons as well. This makes sense because the energetic world is usually reflected in the physical. The following is a list of some of the effects of masturbation on our bodies. It was written by Dr. Newman Lin and is published on his website actionlove.com:

"Over-masturbation results in ADD based upon the fact that semen contains the same fluids found in the brain and spine. The brain and spine fluids are used by the body to form the neurotransmitters acetylcholine, dopamine, serotonin and GABA and to support the central and autonomic nervous communication. When masturbation depletes the fluids in the

brain and spine, you will experience sexual exhaustion due to deficiency of acetylcholine, dopamine, serotonin and GABA. Chronic over-masturbation depletes the brain's acetylcholine, dopamine, serotonin and GABA levels. When their neurons starve, they die. Then, the chronic over-masturbators will continuously suffer. It takes many years to exhaust the brain and nervous systems; naturally, it will take a few months or years to regenerate the neurons to 'heal' the problems."

In other words, masturbation is deadly to our nervous system which in turn affects other systems in our body. In the same way a low vibration is going to affect our vortex of creation which in turn will affect everything else in our life. For the sake of our vibration we should really consider giving up this practice.

Let's move on to another topic, prostitution. This is an area, like masturbation, where there is a great deal of denial amongst us. No one wants to admit it but the data shows that many of us take part in this practice. It is nothing to be ashamed of, our only concern is the effect this practice has on our vibration.

A couple of points, this can seem like a very complicated issue because sex is the highest vibrational act we can do outside of meditation. Therefore it is natural to desire to take part in it as often as possible. The question we need to ask is whether the type of sex we are taking part in raises our vibration or lowers it. I would suggest that acts where money is exchanged for sex are very low vibrational for the simple reason that they are not really free-will consensual acts. Sure both parties are agreeing to it but I would assume most prostitutes would rather be doing something else with their lives and the customers would prefer to not be paying for sex.

This is not to be judgmental of people working in or taking part in the sex trade, it is just a simple observation that if we are serious about raising our vibration we need to put all issues on the table that could jeopardize that quest. It would be a disservice not to explore these taboo subjects and as a result remain stuck in a cycle of low vibrational sexual relationships. Although there are all kinds of sexual dysfunctions in our world that are used to justify all types of behaviors and life choices, it is important to realize we have a unique opportunity to escape the matrix if we want to and create a new earth. No matter the dysfunction, by raising our vibration the condition will correct itself as we are healed by the high vibrational energy of the universe.

Prostitution is said to be the world's oldest profession. This is probably true and many will scoff at the idea that it will go away anytime soon. True, it has been around forever and become kind of mainstream, however, at this point in our history we have the opportunity to raise our vibrations in a way previous generations have not. Prostitution is, I believe, a very low vibrational pursuit that we are being called out of. This way we can align with the highest energies of the universe.

Prostitution, like masturbation, is really a compromise. It is a one-sided act and doesn't involve the free exchange of energy between two participants. Of course there are people who are in a place where they have neither the economic ability nor the desire to quit these practices, and that is fine. This is really for those who are frankly tired of the whole archon agenda and want out fast. Believe me, by foregoing masturbation and the whole sex trade our vibrations will thank us.

2

Possessive Sex

Now onto something less controversial, well not really. To insure that everyone is equally offended, let's look at the issue of possessive sex. This is a term we will use to define most modern day relationships. It is the idea that a particular person is my sexual property. To put it bluntly, monogamy. This view, though touted as evolved, is flawed and keeps us locked into low vibrational sexual relationships. Good luck to anyone attempting to challenge this standard, you will find out the definition of crucifixion. However, it needs to be done. If not we will have little hope of alignment and will continue to be manipulated.

Of course this doesn't mean we should be having multiple partnered anonymous sex all the time. As we allow the high vibrational energy of the universe to work in our lives, sexual issues will take care of themselves. Perhaps we will desire monogamy or even celibacy and that is fine as long as they are not enforced by fear. The point is that we should respect the freedom and autonomy of our partners in this area. To believe otherwise is a very low vibrational belief that fosters an unhealthy attachment to our spouse which only gets worse over time.

I feel bad when I see some who have basically given their autonomy over to a spouse or partner. They seem to have lost their unique spirit and energy each were born with and are now locked into a deeply possessive relationship. The common options are to get out of the relationship (divorce, separation) or to just maintain the status quo and put on a smiling face. Some will covertly cheat on their spouse in a desperate attempt to stay alive energetically. This leads to even more problems if found out. So much is given up in this situation by both partners that the betrayed releases pent up emotions of losing their own identity (energy) and blames the betrayer for not sticking to the deal, which was dysfunctional in the first place.

Possessive sex, like prostitution, is the result of a very disordered view of sexuality. They almost feed off of one another as explained in *Sex at Dawn* by Christopher Ryan and Cacilda Jetha:

" 'To keep body and mind untainted,' explains Walter Houghton in *The Victorian Frame of Mind*, the boy was taught to view women as objects of the greatest respect and even awe. He was to consider nice women (his sister and mother, his future bride) as creatures more like angels than human beings-an image wonderfully calculated not only to dissociate love from sex, but to turn love into worship, and worship of purity.' When not in the mood to worship the purity of his sisters, mother, daughters, and wife, men were expected to purge their lust with prostitutes, rather than threatening familial and social stability by 'cheating' with 'decent women.' Nineteenth-century philosopher Arthur Schopenhauer observed that 'there are 80,000 prostitutes in London alone; and what are they if not sacrifices on the altar of monogamy?'"*

It is time to get smart about sex and let go of any disordered views which not only cause havoc in our lives but, even more importantly, keep us trapped in a low vibrational existence. It is a law of physics that energy cannot be created or destroyed. Sexual energy, in the same way, cannot be repressed. If it is, it will find a way to manifest. Continuing with *Sex at Dawn*:

"In some respects, the sexual mores of Victorian Britain replicated the mechanics of the age-defining steam engine. Blocking the

flow of erotic energy creates ever-increasing pressure which is put to work through short, controlled bursts of productivity. Though he was wrong about a lot, it appears Sigmund Freud got it right when he observed that 'civilization' is built largely on erotic energy that has been blocked, concentrated, accumulated, and redirected."

This brings up many interesting ideas regarding erotic energy and its manipulation. One thing is certain, we should allow this energy to flow in ways that raise our vibrational state. We don't have all the answers yet but a good starting point is by steering clear of masturbation, the sex trade and possessive sex. Once our vibration is raised we should align with new insights on sexuality and grow in an ever greater appreciation of this important gateway to the universe.

It is important to tackle a couple of obvious retorts to the idea that monogamy lowers vibration. The first is that it will lead to sexual chaos and we will begin to devolve into animal-like creatures with no self-control. I would argue we are already there. By focusing on only high vibrational sex, which we will get to in a later chapter, humans would become more evolved, not less. Once aligned with our vortex sex would take a back seat as we begin focusing more on our metaphysical creative powers rather than just our physical creative powers. Ironically, as long as sexuality is repressed the act will continue to play an overexagerrated role in our lives and reap havoc in society and in our families. Alignment is the only answer.

The other complaint is that respecting our partner's sexual freedom would destroy relationships. I concede that relationships would become drastically different than they are today, but that would be a good thing. On the issue of loving your life partner or wife I believe the relationship would become healthier simply by respecting their autonomy and offering truly unconditional love. *Sex at Dawn* continues:

"In the literature of evolutionary psychology, in popular culture, in the tastefully appointed offices of marriage counselors, in religious teachings, in political discourse, and in our own mixed-up lives, lust is often mistaken for love. Perhaps even more insidious and damaging in societies insistent on long-term, sexually exclusive monogamy, the negative form of that statement is also true. The absence of lust is misread as indicating an absence of love."

The bottom line is we need to really reflect on what is true and good in the universe. Even if we are not in a place where we can accept letting go of possessive sex rationally, we should for the sake of raising our vibration and aligning with our vortex keep an open mind when it comes to this issue. However, not everyone is ready to let go of this belief, for it is deeply ingrained in our psyches from thousands of years of religious and cultural programming. But we are dealing more with where we are at this point in our evolution. We need to honestly ask the question of whether this practice serves us at present. Of course it doesn't because any type of attachment is extremely low vibrational. The laws of the universe reflect freedom and non-possessiveness and these laws should be honored in our personal relationships if we truly desire alignment.

Of course the archons would like nothing more than to keep us locked into to the practice of possessive sex because as long as this is the norm for our relationships we will remain stuck in their low vibrational matrix. We will not engage our vortex of creation and benefit from the unconditional and unlimited high vibrational energy of the universe. We will remain defenseless to the archon manipulation and sink deeper and deeper into their matrix. We need to really consider this issue because I understand that for many it is a deal-breaker. However, time is short and humans have some decisions to make if we want to leave a better world for future generations.

3

Religion/Politics

Another area that significantly lowers our vibration are religions, which is ironic because they all claim to help connect us with the creator of the universe. However, this is far from the case. Instead they are probably the most effective tool the archons have to sever our connection with the creative energy of the universe. Religions are essentially designed to deceive us into giving away our energy to "god."

The word "church" comes from the name for the Greek "Circe." Circe was an ancient Greek goddess who would hypnotize men, bring them into her house, and turn them into animals -- taking their minds away, so that they could be slaughtered. She was known as "Mother Circe," and her worship was brought to medieval Scotland, in whose language Circe became "Kirk." The Scottish word "Kirk" becomes "Church" in English.

Many of the symbols used in church help to keep people there in a low vibrational state. The main symbol in the west is the crucifix, which of course depicts a man being executed. The cross also, when condensed, becomes the cube or Ka'ba, located in Mecca, Saudi Arabia, to which a billion Muslims turn to face during their prayers five times a day. The black cube is also an area of focus for Jews, who wear a tefillin bracelet (black cube) around their left arm. The cube also represents the planet Saturn which many refer to as the dark sun.

Though we don't realize it, these symbols are locking us in to the low vibrational energy they represent on a subconscious level. Therefore every time we enter a church or see these symbols, the low vibrational energy is triggered. These vibrational triggers are further reinforced by fear which makes overcoming their energetic effect on our lives difficult. It all leads to a deep planet-wide level of control to insure our vibration remains at a very low level.

To add insult to injury, the "god" we think we are honoring at places of worship turns out to be nothing of the sort. The following is from *The Perception Deception* by David Icke:

"Religion has been the greatest form of mass mind and emotional control. Not religions - but religion, singular. The plural only appears to be the case because the worship of the same deities has been hidden behind different names such as Christianity, Judaism, Islam and Hinduism. There is really only one 'ism', be it Judaism, Catholicism, Hinduism, Buddhism, monotheism, polytheism, fascism, socialism, Conservatism, commercialism or, the collective noun for all them - Bollockism."

According to Icke, religions have a number of goals, which are:

1. *Vampire the energy of the congregations and followers as they focus their attention on Archontic-Saturnic symbols.*
2. *Manipulate people to worship the Demiurge-Archons as god or gods.*
3. *Slam shut the minds of the worshipping masses through rejection of all other possibility beyond the belief system that the religion is peddling.*
4. *Play off religion against religion and faction against faction on the basis of 'my god is the only god' when they are in fact all worshipping the same 'god', or gods.*

We almost have to give the archons credit for the level of manipulation they have managed to pull off. Okay enough praise, now get the fuck out of here you leaching little bastards. We need to end this shit now. Enough is enough! As soon as they are exposed for what they have been doing to control humanity for thousands of years, their time is up. It is like shining a light in a dark cave, the whole place lights up. When people understand their game, its game over.

Another low vibrational aspect of church is the practice of cannibalism. Probably one of the lowest acts a person can do vibrationally is the act of eating the flesh and drinking the blood of another human. This is why Satanists perform animal and human sacrifices. These acts carry such a low vibrational signature that they open the door to dark entities taking a strong foothold in the lives of the participants. I think most Satanists know this and have opened up their souls so much to these entities they are what we could call truly possessed and no longer in full control of their decisions.

Many churches in the same way offer a more covert form of cannibalism using bread and wine as the flesh and blood. The mere act of people giving their consent to cannibalism symbolically is enough to hold them in an extremely low vibrational state. The participant's souls are subtly opened to the vibration of this practice which over time will produce the same results as open cannibalism, the lowering of their vibration.

A spin-off of this is when Christians today are told to give their heart to Jesus spiritually. This practice mirrors the Aztecs who would perform human sacrifices and offer the heart of the victim to "god" physically. In the same way as the covert cannibalism, the covert sacrifice of our heart to "god" symbolically keeps us locked into a low vibration while feeding the archons appetite.

Another way in which religions foster a low vibration in people is by promoting the idea that humans are essentially sinful and that "god" is always ready to punish or forgive them for their sins. The point is that the focus given to the entity "god" (who, again, is not the creator of the universe god) takes the power away from the person and their ascension is determined by an outside force. When in reality the raising of our vibration is determined by our actions (and inactions). Through our free will choices we determine whether we will raise our vibration and align with our vortex or not, thereby attaining "salvation" or the unlimited free high vibrational energy of the universe. The entities worshipped as "god" in religions have nothing to do with this. Their goal is to prevent us from attaining this salvation so we will remain in this low vibrational matrix, which is the only "hell" we should be worried about.

In regards to "prayer," the only control we have is over our own personal vibration. The only help we can give others is that by raising our own vibration they may be inspired to do the same once they see the fruits of aligning with their vortex and being filled with the high vibrational energy of the universe. So what is going on when we offer prayers and sacrifice? Though all prayers offered by religious people have good intentions, the reality is our vibration is significantly lowered anytime we give our power away to another entity acting as an intermediary. In the case of prayer, the entities we are giving our power to are mimicking the creator of the universe. So we are understandably tricked into a cycle of offering our prayer and sacrifice to them which in the end keeps us stuck in a low vibrational state.

This is why many religions use fear (low vibration) of the wrath of "god" if we don't attend their churches and allow our energy to be trawled. This teaching of a wrathful "god" has always caused a little warning siren to go off in my head questioning why they would use fear to get us into church. Well it fits in well which the whole archon vibrational matrix they are trying to create in the world. Lately, though, they have had to lay off the fear-mongering a bit because people began to see through it. The archon agenda is always fluid. They realize we are capable of growth so their goal, since they can't stop this evolution, is to at least make sure the low vibrational box they are trying to contain us in is just a little bigger than we are. Otherwise we would see the manipulation for what it is.

Over time we learn to identify these fear tactics before they paralyze our vibration. However, it is important to remain vigilant and protect ourselves from this type of manipulation, which is widespread in society. Movies like *The Exorcist* must have been a huge boost for the archons and their agenda as the fear factor was raised considerably. More recently a whole slew of exorcism type movies have been released which continue to feed the paranoia. The only "devil" we should be concerned with are the archons who figured that if they can control the problem (devil) and the solution ("god"), then we will remain stuck in their matrix and keep coming to them for "help." The following is more from *The Perception Deception* by David Icke:

"Christians and other religions preach that 'Satan' is a master of deception, but they have been deceived themselves by the very force they warn about. Everything is inverted in true Archon fashion and you have the same force playing the good guy 'God' and the bad guy 'anti-god' under names like Satan, the Devil and Lucifer. No matter if people worship the symbol of the 'good guy', like Jesus, or the 'bad guy', as in Satanism, they are worshipping the same guy in different guises and having their energy trawled and their minds programmed either which way. The Great Deceiver of Christianity has greatly deceived Christians. The mind-scramble goes like this: 'Satan has deceived

people into believing in all other religions - except mine because mine is the only true religion.'"

If we take the necessary steps to raise our vibration help will come in the form of alignment with our vortex and the high vibrational energy of the universe. I would also surmise that truly benevolent entities, which most surely exist in this expansive universe, would have more ability to come to our aid if we are in a high vibrational state. However, help from any entities should not be our focus. That is something that will happen naturally if we are resonating at a similar vibration as these entities.

I hate to say it but most religious leaders are being used by the archons to help keep humanity from attaining this alignment. These leaders facilitate lowering the vibration of themselves as well as their congregation so our energy can be trawled by their true masters. At this point I can feel some religious people getting offended, and that is good. If there is any truth to the manipulation taking place through religions, people are smart enough to pick up on it. If there is no truth and it is truly the creator of the universe who is demanding these prayers and sacrifices, people will pick up on that as well. We should at least consider the alternative view that things are not as they seem. Then at least our faith will be tested and grow stronger if true.

Churches and places of worship, though they look attractive and inviting, turn out to be more like roach motels which may provide comfort and rest for a period. Then as time passes on slowly our energetic bodies are eaten away until we are too weak to resist. Yes, Circe is alive and well in our modern day and age. That is the operation the archons have been involved in for thousands of years and it is time for it to stop.

Politics, like religions, is used to divide people into groups. "Divide and conquer" the old saying goes. And so religions, political parties, etc. essentially keep people arguing (low vibration) about things that in the end are of very little consequence to our everyday lives. Can you imagine what would happen if rather than fighting over political and religious ideologies people would come together and meditate for just five minutes a week. The world would change. That is a good example of how much more powerful high vibrations are than low vibrations. Just five minutes would go a long way in healing the week-long arguing, wars and proselytizing.

Politics is a valuable tool for the archons because it keeps people in perpetual argument over every issue. As long as we are stuck in these low vibrational arguments we will just be spinning our wheels when what we need to be focusing on is raising our vibrations and spinning our vortexes of creation, sucking the high vibrational energy of the universe into this world. Then the solutions for many of the issues we are working to solve politically will manifest automatically. We should come to terms with the fact that the answers to our most pressing social problems will only come when we are in alignment with the universe. Then they will flow naturally, but as long as we are arguing politically the spicket is off and we are exacerbating these problems.

Politics, like religion, also allows people to be manipulated, lowering the vibration of the entire planet. This manipulation is done by presenting two choices which are both controlled by the archons. When this happens, people are given a false sense of freedom when in actuality the low vibrational plans for wars, economic crashes, and ultimately keeping people divided into the haves and the have not's can continue without opposition since both parties are on board. This is a reflection of what is happing in religions. People are given two choices which are both controlled by the same evil. Therefore we live with a false sense of freedom in many areas of our lives. The archons have learned that the best prison is the one where you can't see the bars.

One of the most useful political tools, as mentioned in the introduction, is problem, reaction, solution. To create the change they desire in the world, be it more surveillance of citizens, new wars, or less freedom, archons often will create a related problem. People will react to the problem in what is usually a predictable way and a solution, already planned out, will be presented. In this way the world we live is being slowly steered into the future the archons want to create. If political leaders were to come out and say they want to limit people's freedoms and institute a police state, obviously we would react in a negative way. However, by covertly creating a problem, we end up begging them for the same solution. It has worked time and again so why would the archons change it. It is important for us to at least be aware that this is how they operate. We should not worry too much about it (low vibration) or get caught up in conspiracies. Rather as we raise our vibration the ability of the archons to continue to manipulate us in this way will be greatly weakened and ultimately diminish.

4

Wheat/Recreational Drugs

Continuing on with things that lower our vibration is wheat. This grain is a huge factor in keeping us in a very low vibrational state, which is probably why it is used in the church "sacrifice." The effect of wheat on our physical bodies is a reflection of what is going on vibrationally when we consume it. Wheat causes obesity, diabetes and many other ailments. It is also highly addictive. If there were a conspiracy to lower the vibration of people across the planet, wheat would be the perfect weapon.

Eating foods made with wheat, about 80 percent of what is in the grocery store, is like a slow death keeping us mired in a low vibrational muck. People who have given up wheat have seen amazing results. Diseases disappear, massive amounts of weight is lost, and mental clarity result. Dr. William Davis offers the following observation in his best-selling book *Wheat Belly:*

"If this thing called wheat is such a problem, then removing it should yield outsized and unexpected benefits. Indeed, that is the case. As a cardiologist who sees and treats thousands of patients at risk for heart disease, diabetes, and the myriad destructive effects of obesity, I have personally observed protuberant, flop-over-the-belt belly fat vanish when my patients eliminated wheat from their diets, with typical weight loss totaling 20, 30, or 50 pounds just within the first few months. Rapid and effortless weight loss is usually followed by health benefits that continue to amaze me even today after having witnessed this phenomenon thousands of times.

I've seen dramatic turnarounds in health, such as the thirty-eight-year-old woman with ulcerative colitis facing colon removal who was cured with wheat elimination-colon intact. Or the twenty-six-year-old man, incapacitated and barely able to walk because of joint pain, who experienced complete relief and walked and ran freely again after taking wheat off the menu.

Extraordinary as these results may sound, there is ample scientific research to implicate wheat as the root cause of these conditions-and to indicate that removal of wheat can reduce or relieve symptoms entirely. You will see that we have unwittingly traded convenience, abundance, and low cost for health with wheat bellies, bulging thighs, and double chins to prove it."

The physical and psychological benefits of giving up wheat are reflected in our vibration. As we give up this grain our vibration will naturally raise allowing us to align with our vortex. I hate to sound repetitive here but all these steps lead to this same end, alignment with the high vibrational energy of the universe. To think that our physical habits and actions have no bearing on our metaphysical bodies is naive and continuing with this belief will keep us perpetually trapped in the low vibrational matrix of the archons. Everything we do in our lives will either aid us in our evolution or suppress us. Wheat suppresses our vibration on a massive scale and avoiding it is key to our alignment.

Again, we could get into other dietary tips but none of them would kick start our vibration anywhere near as much as the simple act of avoiding wheat. And the archons know this otherwise governments and religions would not make such a concerted effort to promote wheat consumption (food pyramid). Even Dr. Davis, who is as mainstream as you can get, said in an interview on YouTube entitled *Wheat Murder:*

"If there were a conspiracy, this thing called wheat is perfectly crafted to ruin health, to cause hypertension, heart disease, diabetes, and thousands of other conditions all while you reap the benefits of selling more drugs, selling more procedures. I was not real hot on the whole conspiracy notion until after Wheat Belly came out and hit the book stores when I found out that a lot of the wheat lobby is paid for by the diabetes drug industry. That even surprised me that the diabetes drug industry is paying for a lot of the lobbying efforts promoting 'healthy' whole grains."

Once we kiss this grain goodbye, our diet will no longer be as big a factor in lowering our vibration. Sure we will always grow in our understanding of our bodies and how to keep it healthy but we will no longer be putting what amounts to rat poison into our systems on a daily basis. Just like the concoction given to Mia Farrow's character in *Rosemary's Baby*, wheat keeps our health and vibration suppressed, which in turn feeds the entities trying to leach off of us.

Another substance we should avoid taking if we are serious about raising our vibration is recreational drugs. Raising our vibration requires sound mind and body. Recreational drugs distort our mental and physical selves and causes confusion. Ultimately, while this can be fun for a while, these drugs can make it very difficult to maintain the focus necessary to appreciate the high vibrational energy of the universe. We need all of our minds and bodies operating at a very high level to be able to process this universal energy. Drugs tend to make us less focused and less able to maintain the vibration necessary to facilitate this process of alignment.

In the same way that wheat is the perfect weapon to ruin people's physical health, recreational drugs are the perfect weapon to ruin the health of a society. This has been used time and again since the Opium Wars between Great Britain and China in the 1800's when the Chinese Emperor banned the trade of most European goods. Europeans began to smuggle opium into the country which of course caused addiction to the drug to skyrocket. It wasn't long after that the British were given Hong Kong along with five treaty ports.

This same drama plays out in American cities and it is documented that our own CIA has a role in supplying drugs to this country. Again, recreational drugs make a population more docile and therefore more easily manipulated. They are less likely to stand up to their government, or if they do their protest will be less effective.

Of course the term recreational drugs covers a wide range of substances so we should distinguish a bit amongst them. Marijuana and alcohol would of course be considered lightweight drugs. My personal view is that alcohol in moderation has a neutral effect on our vibration. To me alcohol is like television, as long as we don't overindulge we should not spend our focus on stopping these practices. Of course we should only put good things in our body and mind. If we are going to have a drink, we should make sure it is high quality. Similarly with television, we should try to avoid shows that lower our vibration.

Just a quick aside note on television, though I love *Seinfeld,* I have a problem with the whole "fake laugh" in sit-coms. It is a type of subliminal programming which I honestly find disturbing. I'm not sure if this is true or not but I heard those laugh noises actually were recorded in the 1950's which means, as my daughter pointed out recently, that most of those people are probably dead now. I just find it creepy and unnecessary. If something is truly funny, people will laugh. Can you imagine if a standup comic tried to play fake laughs? They would immediately be identified as a fraud. However, we accept this practice on sit-coms. So television and film is really a blank canvas which artists can use for good or ill.

In this day and age it is unrealistic to even try to give up television since it has become such an integral part of our society. And being that it is essentially neutral, there is no reason to justify giving it up. Movies are awesome entertainment and can cause us to reflect on life in profound ways. As our vibration is raised in other ways, we will automatically become less interested in programming that does not resonate with us and gravitate towards film and television that will aid us in our alignment, or at the very least have no effect at all.

Now back to the issue at hand. Though I don't judge people who smoke marijuana, for me personally it would be a detriment to alignment simply because it is a hallucinogen and would serve more to confuse things. Of course the other drugs are highly addictive and would definitely lower our vibration. The truth is, as we raise our vibration the desire to experiment and look for fulfillment with recreational drugs will disappear. There is no drug that even comes close to the high vibrational energy of the universe. Using them will actually inhibit the process of receiving this energy so it is best we leave the drugs to the sick.

It is important to note that there are many who hold the belief that ayahuasca, a concoction which is said to release or activate DMT in our pineal gland, actually helps us in raising our awareness of the interconnectedness of the universe. This is possible and I am not an expert in this area. In general if we follow all the steps to raise our vibration outlined in this book there should be no need for additional substances to attain alignment.

5

Anger/Violence/Fear

The acts of anger and violence are uniquely damaging to our vibrational state in that they create a cycle that is very hard to break. Justified anger, of which there is much, is especially bad due to the fact that it seems right but has deadly vibrational consequences. Though it is extremely difficult we should by a sheer act of the will raise our vibration when we are confronted with anger or violence.

What does anger do to our vibration? Japanese researcher, Dr. Masaru Emoto, has made some astounding discoveries regarding this. He has written books illustrating how human thought and emotion changes the vibrational structure of water. Dr. Emoto attaches words and other things to jars of water which are then frozen very quickly. He then photographs the frozen water crystals. The crystals seem to take on different structures depending on which words were attached to the jar of water. For example, a jar with the words love and appreciation attached to it create a beautiful snowflake-like crystal. In contrast, a jar with the words "you make me sick, I want to kill you" attached to it produces an eerie figure with what appears to be a gun.

Dr. Emoto's work provides a snapshot into the power of our thoughts and emotions on our vibration. His work reminds us that we need to be vigilant about what we allow to enter our vibrational field because it will end up affecting the degree to which we will align with our vortex. Anger, violence and fear are three of the worst things we can do to our vibration because they are usually cyclical, meaning that once we give in to them, it is very hard to escape. Almost like a negative vortex.

It is a good idea to steer clear from those who have anger or provoke anger in us, whether it be family members, friends or co-workers. It is more important to focus on our vibration. Once we do this and our vortex kicks into gear, those angry people will just fade away from our existence. No need to worry about dealing with them because the universe will take care of it for us. The low vibration of anger simply cannot function around the higher vibrations of love. Sure there is a chance the angry person will raise their vibration after our example and great but that is for them to decide, not us.

Violence, we should note, is not just physical but can also be economic, verbal and energetic. Personally, for me to overcome this in my life I had to be attacked in the worst way and was filled with such anger that I had no choice but to raise my vibration. Otherwise the anger would have consumed me. Raising our vibration with love is the only solution when confronted with extremely low vibrational anger. Just to clarify, this doesn't mean physically showing your love to an angry person. Though there are times when a hug may be in order, what is more important is our personal vibration. As we are filled with the high vibrational energy of the universe, it will overflow into those around us.

When I was confronted with anger, hatred and what can only be described as evil by someone who was very close to me, my only salvation was to raise my vibration through meditation. When we are attacked financially and in other vindictive ways, it is no doubt the worst thing a person can go through outside of a war. I had never experienced such a low vibrational attack and the fact that it came from someone I trusted made it that much worse. I'm sure we have all experienced this to some degree.

But just as gold is purified through fire, we can use times of low vibrational attack as a purification of our own selves. Ironically, these trials can end up being our biggest blessings if we use them as a catalyst to raise our vibration and align with our vortex. The people doing the attack often take the role as Gollum in the *Lord of the Rings,* inadvertently destroying the evil they promoted. Darth Vader also comes to mind when he chunked the emperor into the abyss.

Sometimes these dark nights are what we need in order to progress vibrationally. I think this is what Esther Hicks means when she talks about contrast. The bad experiences help us to clarify what it is we do want. The worse the experience, the greater experience we can create as a contrast. I know it is difficult to see things in this way but this is what it means to be a conscious creator. We have the power to create our own lives and low vibrational experiences will aid us along to way to create a better world. Once they are overcome there is nothing another person can do to bring us down, it becomes metaphysically impossible.

My sense is that African Americans have a naturally strong vibration due to the unfathomable evils they and their ancestors overcame during slavery and segregation. That purification has been passed on through generations and has ironically become a source of strength and courage in the descendants of those who were treated as property and denied their dignity. Perhaps that is why African Americans are widely acknowledged to have a greater connection with the universe, which is naturally expressed through music and other art forms. This high vibrational residue seems to be imprinted on their soul. They have been purified by fire and the result is gold.

As we do the work of raising our vibration, we will all be filled with the high vibrational energy of the universe, which could also be called infinite love. As we are filled it will automatically overflow into our families and relationships but until we are overflowing it may be a good idea to limit the amount of time we spend around those who may be a detriment to this alignment.

I mentioned in the introduction the hive mind, which is what I call the control system of the archons. This is a key point because they really can't control us overtly. That would go against the universal law of free will. What they can do is get us to control one another. As an example, let's say our world is a group of ten people sitting in a room. There is a door in the room but we have all come to believe that evil lies behind that door and have never opened it. This belief is reinforced by fear that if we attempt to open the door we will suffer eternally (big red flag). Then one person decides to get up and open the door. That person is immediately attacked by others because they have been conditioned (programmed) a certain way through fear. It really is like a prison without bars.

The same is true in our lives. There are many people in this world who are what could be called conscious creators. These people know there is more to this life than meets the eye. They refuse to go along with the program and are singled out as potential roadblocks for the archon agenda. The method used for dealing with these "mavericks" is through the hive mind. They usually are attacked and discouraged by those around them who are largely unconscious and have become archon tools.

There are many levels to this control but they all work towards the same end - preventing us from alignment with the universe. This is why archons prefer hierarchical structures, because they make it easier for the few to control the many. Of course the talking points come from the highest levels of the religious, government and media hierarchy which are then filtered down into the masses. At that point we pretty much take over and control one another. This is the hive mind in action. If a conscious creator reaches a high enough level on the world stage and poses a serious threat to the agenda, they are usually dealt with in more permanent ways. JFK comes to mind.

By raising our vibration, any anger or hive mind attacks that surround us will necessarily disappear since, again, a low vibrational energy cannot co-exist with high vibrational energy. This is such an important concept it is worth repeating a hundred times until we grasp it. It is similar to the idea that whatever we are thinking and feeling we will attract in our life, though I believe understanding how to raise our vibration is a much more powerful truth when it comes to manifesting our desires.

The key to overcoming anger or hatred is love and kindness. The following story comes from *Don't Die with Your Music Still in You* by Serena Dyer:

"My dad loves to say, 'If you have a choice to either be right or kind, choose kindness.' I remember him demonstrating just that at a restaurant we go to frequently on Maui. However, none of us liked the waitress there, who seemed to make it her personal goal to say no to almost every request we had. Dad could have argued on our behalf-asked to see her manager, demanded she give us better service, or just stopped taking us there. But he was more interested in being kind than right. So one night he decided to make a change. 'I am going to turn her around with kindness,' he said. The next time we went to this restaurant, dad

started off by asking the woman how her day was, where she was from, and if she had any family on the island. Then he gave her a genuine compliment on her new hairdo. When he asked for avocado on his salad this time around, she didn't object - she was happy to bring him the extra item, at no additional charge."

Fear is also a huge factor in the suppression of our vibrational state. Governments use fear as a tactic to keep people in line. A good example of this is the terror alerts that were instituted shortly after 9/11. Everyone was scared to death of another terror attack and voluntarily gave up many of their liberties in exchange for the government's "security." As I write these words the news is reporting an Ebola outbreak that threatens to quarantine people if it is not contained. We will see what comes of it but archons do know how to keep their manipulations going. If people begin to protest against the wars, they simply move onto another tactic of control where they will not be resisted. It is really like a game to them and we need to understand their game and put an end to it. The only way this will happen is through raising our vibrations and alignment.

Religions also use fear in the same way. As long as there is a devil boogeyman out there, people will flock to religion for salvation. They will surrender much of their common sense in order to be saved from burning for an eternity. Eternal "security" if you will.

As long as we allow the archon-controlled governments and religions to suppress our vibration using fear tactics, we will have great difficulty progressing as a people. Fear is a sure fire way to shut down our vortex of creation and turn us into impotent spirits that can be easily manipulated in mass. As long as our vibration is kept low we will be docile pawns in the hands of the new world order desired by the archons.

Of course the answer to fear is to raise our vibration by not being afraid of anything, what good will that do anyway? Once we align with our vortex of creation and see our power as infinite consciousness, all fear (and the archons promoting it) will dissipate and the world will change.

B. Things That Raise Vibration

6

Non-Possessive Sex

Ok, now that we have focused a bit on things that lower our vibration, it is time to get to the good stuff - things that raise our vibration. First among these is non-possessive sex. In the same way possessive sex lowers vibration, non-possessive sex is a gateway to a very high vibrational existence. We should all decide to get smart about sex and reap the benefits of this practice, without all the shame.

Of course many will scoff at the idea of non-possessive sex as "swinging" or "promiscuity." But any attack on the idea of non-possessive sex is archon inspired. The reason being that they know the energetic and vibrational power of any free-willed consensual sex. They also know how repressed sexual energy wreaks havoc on our vibration thereby cutting off our connection with the universe.

At its core masturbation, prostitution and possessive sex are not consensual because they are all metaphysically one-sided. The reality is that technically these acts are not even sex which is a Synergistic Energy eXchange. For something to be synergistic there needs to be two willing participants.

The real power of high vibrational non-possessive sex is the effect this has on our chakras. The heart chakra, which is associated with love, is by far the biggest factor when it comes to alignment. When it is activated it will pull in more of this high vibrational energy of the universe than we will know what to do with. Non-possessive sex is a powerful way to engage this chakra and get it producing for us. This is truly "making love" and will transform our lives. The other low-vibrational forms of sex we have discussed do not engage this heart vortex, I am sorry to say. So we really need to take this into account when choosing our sexual activities.

Suffice it to say then that masturbation, prostitution, and possessive sex are not synergistic. They are more a one-sided energy suck which can be detrimental to our vibration. Non-possessive sex on the other hand is a true energetic exchange between two people who respect the free will and autonomy of each other. The vibrational difference between the practices is profound.

Archons also realize that, when mixed with fear, sex can become a very powerful tool of control. They know that if they can pull off the trick of restricting our access to high vibrational sex while at the same time stimulating our desires, many dysfunctions will result. As long as they are making the rules about sex we will be stuck in a rut of shame and desire never fulfilled. The following is from *Sex at Dawn:*

"Like the Victorians, most contemporary Western societies inflate the inherent value of sex by restricting supply ('Good girls don't') and inflating demand (Girls Gone Wild). This process leads to a distorted vision of just how important sex actually is. Yes, sex is essential, but it's not something that must always be taken so seriously. Think of food, water, oxygen, shelter, and all the other elements of life crucial to survival and happiness but that don't figure in our day-to-day thinking unless they become unavailable. A reasonable relaxation of moralistic social codes making sexual satisfaction more easily available would also make it less problematic."

In other words, sex should not be the hornet's nest it has become. The attack on this area of our lives by the archons should tip us off to what is really going on. Sex is a huge factor in our vibration. If we were to figure this out and learn how to use it properly, there would be mass alignment across the planet. Archons know this and are doing everything they can to keep us from realizing this. For them to succeed, sex needs to remain "dirty" because as soon as we realize it is not and we can use it to raise our vibration and align with the universe, their little low vibrational orgy is over.

The practice of non-possessive sex in no way undermines the idea of having a partner who shares a special place in our life. It actually will strengthen the relationship because it would be truly unconditional love. Rather than avoiding how we truly feel, couples would have the permission to be honest with one another about their desires. This would facilitate learning and growth rather than fear-induced repression which seems to be the norm. Again, from *Sex at Dawn:*

"Couples might find that the only route to preserving or rediscovering intensity (energy) reminiscent of their early days and nights requires confronting the open, uncertain sky together. They may find themselves having their most meaningful, intimate conversations if they dare to talk about the true nature of their feelings. We don't mean to suggest these will be easy conversations. They won't be. There are zones where it's always going to be difficult for men and women to understand one another, and sexual desire is one of them. Many women will find it difficult to accept that men can so easily dissociate

sexual pleasure from emotional intimacy, just as many men will struggle to understand why these two obviously separate (to them) issues are so often intertwined for many women."

The practice of non-possessive sex is infinitely more psychologically healthy than the possessive version. Our sexual energy would no longer be repressed out of fear of the repercussions, rather it would flow freely as it was meant to through sexual experiences. This is reflected in our vibrational health as well. The more our energy flows the higher our vibration. As we grow in our practice of non-possessive sex, our vibration will continue to raise. Our vortex of creation will respond to this by picking up momentum and making every new day a more powerful creation of ourselves.

One quick note about sex. As we raise our vibration through our thoughts and feelings, let the universe (from our vortex of creation) come to us. It should be a process of ease but we need to trust in the process and give it some space to work. It will if we release ourselves from the habit of trying to force it.

The metaphysical reality is that we are all one and the practice of non-possessive sex is closer to this reality. As we let go of our attachments we will be better able to experience this oneness thereby raising our vibration. Attachment of any kind only serves to lower it making us less engaged with the creative universe. As Yoda counsels Anakin: "Attachment leads to jealousy, the shadow of greed that is. Train yourself to let go of everything you fear to lose."

7

Meditation

Meditation is key to raising our vibration. It provides the foundation for us to communicate with the universe and come to understand our purpose. In a world of noise and distraction, meditation grounds us to what is truly important - raising our vibration and aligning with our vortex of creation. From this everything else in our life will flow effortlessly and the world will change. Meditation is especially powerful when two or more people are involved, maybe because it makes us more focused in our practice.

Meditation is our connection with the universe. Our lives can be complicated with all the choices we feel we need to make. Once we raise our vibration and align with our vortex the answers flow. Solutions from our vortex lead us into the best possible life based on our desires and beliefs.

The archons know this which is why we are being inundated with stimulating images in movies, television, and computer games. It is a desperate attempt to keep us focused on our five sense reality rather than finding our power within. They know that once we do this their control over our lives and vibration will be greatly diminished. Therefore it is imperative that we be constantly stimulated.

Of course there are many benefits to modern technology such as the spread of information and ideas that contribute to our evolution. However, this needs to be balanced with meditation, especially for kids today who are uniquely vulnerable to having their humanity subverted by over exposure to a virtual reality digital universe, or matrix.

And it is not an unbearable burden to incorporate meditation into children's lives. Committing to just a few minutes a day will act as an antidote to the countless hours spent on computer games, TV, etc. It will help to maintain their connection to the universe which is particularly vulnerable in the early years of human development. The archons know this and are doing all they can to turn young humans into floundering chattel they can easily control and manipulate in later years.

There are documented accounts of schools that have implemented the regular practice of meditation during the day. The results are improved test scores, less discipline problems, and most importantly students who are better able to deal with the stresses of everyday life.

In my own family my children and I meditate every night for five or ten minute periods. It doesn't take much and the results are well worth the effort. We usually start after dinner and the practice helps to set the tone for the evening. Once finished we usually find ourselves in meaningful discussion about how our day went. Overall it helps all of us to focus on what we need to get done each evening and also gives us the message that it is okay to just relax and unwind.

Morning meditation is also very powerful and my son and I do it as often as possible. Of course meditating in the morning helps to begin the day on a very high vibration. It helps to release a little stress each time so that all the daily challenges we encounter do not become overwhelming.

Mentally, meditation helps to release emotions from past events and to focus the mind on the present. A term used for this process is psychological unloading and the long-term effect of this is a more peaceful disposition and less psychological dysfunction. This is a great boost for our vibration because traumatic memories trapped in our subconscious are a serious obstacle to our alignment and need to be disposed of. These memories are excess baggage we have no reason to be carrying around. They weigh us down on our life journey making it more difficult than it should be.

Everyone has pent up emotional trauma to varying degrees and it is not really necessary to identify the root cause of them. Regular meditation, along with the overall raising of our vibration by other means, will cause these emotions to rise to the surface. This will often happen when we are in the dream state. Once these repressed memories enter into our conscious minds, they can be released effortlessly and the process of alignment will have cleared a major hurdle.

The practice of meditation also helps with relaxation, releasing stress, improving concentration, gaining insight and self-discipline. Additionally, it is used for healing purposes and is becoming more common in medicine as a way to reduce pain and stress. Many diseases can be linked to stress and, therefore, reducing it can increase overall health.

Eastern medicine teaches that there are seven main energy centers in the body called chakras. Meditation is used to open and release blockages in these chakras that are believed to be linked to disease. This is similar to psychological unloading, however, many of our most traumatic memories are stored in different areas of the body, which are associated with the different chakra energy centers. These centers definitely have an impact on the health of the area of the body in which it is located.

The flow of energy through our seven chakras is very important because the better that energy is flowing, the higher our vibration. And, all together, the higher our vibration, the faster our vortex of creation will spin bringing us into alignment.

All health, love peace and prosperity will flow abundantly once aligned with our vortex. We will no longer need to worry about our future, the only thing we need to be focused on is keeping our vibration raised. Meditation works in conjunction with all the other areas of our lives. If our vibration is lowered from anger, masturbation, wheat, religion, or possessive sex, our meditation will not be as powerful.

The level of tranquility we feel in our meditation is a good indicator of our overall vibrational state. If we are not at peace during our meditation there may be an area of our lives where our vibration is being suppressed. As we learn more and more each day to raise our vibration the results in our meditation should be peace, rest, and focus. Our vibration works in a synergistic way and as we withdraw from all the things that lower our vibration simultaneously, the results are amazing.

Meditation also teaches us that we have access to the universe at all times. We can meditate wherever we are. We don't need to be in a certain setting or with certain people. And it is free, as are all the best things in the universe. The following is from *Don't Die with Your Music Still in You* by Serena Dyer:

"I went to a Christian school as a kid, and I remember my friends thinking that you could only talk to God when you had your hands folded in church. I tried to tell a boy in my class that I talked to God all the time, and he said I was lying. I was very upset and told my parents about this, and they said that I should try to teach my classmate that God was everywhere and could be talked to by anyone at any time. It was then I began to understand that I was 'different,' and so were my parents. They encouraged me to ask questions and find my own truth, rather than blindly adhere to what was written down in a book, what I was taught, or what the current fad was. I realized that the only way to find those inner truths was to go within, and that meant turning down the sound in my head."

As we do this, turn down the sound in our head, our vibration will raise higher and higher. This is the most fundamental way we can insure that our vortex is engaged and producing for us. When it comes to alignment, meditation is the key that opens the door to the universe.

8

The Great
Outdoors/Pets

In a similar way that meditation helps us to connect with the universe in a deep way for a few minutes at a time, when in nature we have the opportunity to connect as well. Mountains, trees, oceans and animals are all extremely high vibrational if we have the eyes to see it. The more time we spend outdoors contemplating these creations, the more they will begin to impact our personal vibration.

The key is we need to be conscious of the high energy of these things in nature. Sure we see a tree with our eyes, but the metaphysical reality is that the tree is alive with energy that is there for us to take advantage of. I picture trees and other things in nature as having a high vibrating golden energy. This is what I believe they would look like if we were looking at them from the quantum physics level.

And where does all of this "golden" energy come from? The sun of course. Here we are really trying to scratch the surface of the mechanics of our galaxies and universe. It is impossible to overestimate the role of the stars to the life in their respective spheres of influence. Energy from our sun permeates everything in our lives and brings life and high vibrational energy to our planet. And this same scenario is playing out across the universe. Here we are really touching upon the nature who we are.

We will use the term god even though it has been abused endlessly by the archons to sever our connection with the creative source of the universe. This source, or "god," is available to all of us and is governed, as are the archons, by universal laws. I would never claim to have a full understanding of these laws and anyone who does is part of the archon hive mind. However, it doesn't take a rocket scientist to make the connection that if the suns play such an important role in our physical world, chances are they play just as important a role in our metaphysical vibrational universe.

So what does this mean? Just as trees, oceans, animals, and mountains help to raise our vibration when we are around them, the sun deserves pride of place when it comes to our observation of the energy around us. It is truly the source of many of these things in nature and without it we would not even be here. Does this mean we should worship the sun? Of course not, we are "worshipping" (stupid word, I know) our connection to that which is the creative source of the universe. Of course we are part of that creative source but will never be fully realized as long as we are cut off from it. And the way we restore the connection is by raising our vibration in order to realign with that source.

Being in nature and the outdoors is a huge boost to this realignment. This doesn't necessarily mean even being outdoors. As I sit and write these words I am appreciating the energy of the trees outside my window. Just looking at the fig tree loaded with ripe fruit gives me a vibrational boost. Even if we aren't within sight of nature, we can still vibrationally connect with it. Perhaps this was what Oscar Wilde meant when he wrote, "Wilderness begins in the mind." As long as we are able to make the connection with something through our thoughts and feeling, we can benefit from its high vibration and feed on it if you will. Of course it is good as much as possible to spend time in nature and feast on the schmorgasborg that awaits us there vibrationally.

One of my biggest vibrational boosts comes from being around the centuries old oak trees in New Orleans City Park. There is something about the energy of these old trees that is nourishing. They have been around since before all the man-made interference of cell phones and other electromagnetic distortions in the atmosphere and are a storehouse of pure high vibrational energy. My son and I sometimes meditate under an old oak and the energy is palpable. He actually will rush to finish his mile bike ride before me to spend a few extra minutes in meditation under the old oak. Children are unique in that they can see more clearly sources of high vibrational energy as long as they are given the chance to connect with the universe through regular meditation. In the same way as planets are drawn to the stars in a gravitational orbit, children are drawn to these sources of energy. We all are to a certain extent.

Pets are also a huge vibrational boost. They are our loyal companions but also don't carry around all the negative karma humans can. Animals in general seem to have a naturally high vibration that we can pick up on. Esther Hicks describes this in *The Vortex:*

"While animals do experience contrast, and they do vibrationally ask for improved conditions, they remain more often in alignment with their Broader Perspective than humans do. It is possible to

be actively involved in sifting through contrast, as humans are, and to deliberately guide your thoughts into resonance with your Broader Perspective and experience the benefit of being an active creator at the same time that you are in the state of allowing. And while the animals of your planet are an important source of food for each other and for humans, the greatest value they bring to life on planet Earth is the Vibrational balance they provide, as they are extensions of Source Energy and remain predominantly in alignment with that Energy. Humans and animals make a very nice combination, just as you knew you would."

My greatest love of the outdoors is without a doubt the ocean. It is a mass of extremely high vibrational energy that overtakes all of my senses when I am close to it: sight, smell, sound, and touch. The ocean holds a deep attraction for me since I had the good fortune of growing up fishing on the beaches of the Gulf of Mexico. Sure I was focused on catching speckled trout, redfish and flounder, but vibrationally there was a connection being made with the energy in that big body of water that has never left me. I think this is what people mean when they say it is always a good day fishing, catching is a bonus. There is a deep truth here regarding our connection with the natural world, our souls are being fed during these outings.

These connections made with nature will never leave any of us. They are there all around us for our benefit. Most of us have subconsciously known this all our lives and been drawn to these things. Now is the time to more consciously use these things to massively raise our vibration and align with our vortex.

9

Exercise

Exercise is another great way to raise our vibration. In the same way as meditation can be used to get our chakras (energy body) flowing, exercise gets our blood flowing. For this reason it is sometimes called a meditation for the body. Exercise leads to good health which is the physical manifestation of raising our vibration because it reflects what we want to happen in relation to our vortex. We want everything flowing and healthy. Energy at a high vibration flows whereas energy at a low vibration is stagnant.

This doesn't mean of course we need to go overboard with exercise and do things that are unpleasant for us. Though we want to push our limits, it is best to start with something enjoyable such as stretching and walking or running outdoors.

This is a great way to kill two birds with one stone. Not only are we getting our physical body flowing but we are also benefiting vibrationally from being in nature.

Nothing against P90X but that is not what I am talking about when I say exercise. For exercise to raise our vibration it should be fun. If not it could end up being a net negative. Maybe some people need "boot camps" for motivation but I have found just being in nature is motivation enough. Combining nature with exercise is perfect because it gives us an excuse to spend extended periods of time outdoors.

The goal here is to keep our exercise routine going. This means we should focus on activities we enjoy. If we do it is less likely we will become discouraged and give up. This is why I only meditate with the kids for five to ten minutes each day. This is something they can handle. If I try to up the ante to 20 or 30 minutes they would probably rebel because it would become a drudgery for them. The key with all these things is to find a balance that is sustainable. Discouragement only benefits the archons because it keeps us from taking the steps that will lead to a gradual raising of our vibration, which is organic and grows in a natural way, not in extreme leaps and bounds.

As we incorporate any of the suggestions in this book, including exercise, we should keep this in mind. As we get used to doing the things that raise our vibration we will receive feedback from our vortex that will guide us into how we can effortlessly keep the process going in a natural way. We will also be challenged to push ourselves a little more everyday as we become stronger in our vibration.

In the area of exercise and its relationship to our flow of energy, we could learn from the Chinese practice of qigong (life energy cultivation). Qigong practice will do more to get our energy moving again than perhaps any other methodology. The following is a synopsis of its origins and practice from Wikipedia:

"Qigong is a practice of aligning body, breath, and mind for health, meditation, and martial arts training. With roots in Chinese medicine, philosophy, and martial arts, qigong is traditionally viewed as a practice to cultivate and balance qi (chi) or what has been translated as 'life energy'.

According to Daoist, Buddhist, and Confucian philosophy, respectively, qigong allows access to higher realms of awareness, awakens one's 'true nature', and helps develop human potential.

Qigong practice typically involves moving meditation, coordinating slow flowing movement, deep rhythmic breathing, and calm meditative state of mind. Qigong is now practiced throughout China and worldwide for recreation, exercise and relaxation, preventive medicine and self-healing, complementary and alternative medicine, meditation and self-cultivation, and training for martial arts.

Over the centuries, a diverse spectrum of qigong forms developed in different segments of Chinese society. Traditionally, qigong training has been esoteric and secretive, with knowledge passed from adept master to student in lineages that maintain their own unique interpretations and methods. Although the practice of qigong was prohibited during the Cultural Revolution of the 1960s; it was once again allowed after 1976; and disparate approaches were merged and popularized, with emphasis shifted away from traditional philosophy, spiritual attainment, and folklore, and increasingly to health benefits, traditional medicine and martial arts applications, and a scientific perspective. Since a 1999 crackdown, practice of qigong in China has been restricted. Over the same period, interest in qigong has spread, with millions of practitioners worldwide."

Practices such as qigong, tai chi and yoga are a blend of meditation with exercise and can be powerful boosts to our vibration. The key, however, is to begin with an exercise with which we feel comfortable and find enjoyable. As our vibration is raised we should just keep an open mind about these and other advanced eastern practices and incorporate them into our routine if we feel drawn to them. The indicator that we are ready to incorporate these practices into our daily routine, again, will be whether we enjoy them or not.

Our process of alignment truly is like exercise. The more we raise our vibration (exercise), the faster our vortex of creation will spin (strength). This process will take us to new levels vibrationally and strengthen our vortex. We will become stronger conscious creators as we progress higher and higher in our alignment. In the same way our physical bodies will grow in strength as exercise becomes part of our daily routine. Maybe some people will enjoy training for and completing a triathlon. As long as we follow our bliss or enjoyment, whatever exercise we do will be a boost to our overall vibrational state.

Of course exercise alone does not automatically lead to a high vibration as there are too many other factors involved. However, in conjunction with the other steps laid out, it is an important area that deserves our attention if we are truly interested in alignment.

10

Love/Forgiveness

Love and forgiveness is the most important key to raising our vibration. If we follow all the other steps and do not have these, our vibration will hit a ceiling and not go any higher. Love is all there is, everything else is an illusion. The creative universe (god, us) is pure love at its highest vibration. All the other things we do to raise our vibration will complement love and forgiveness but none of them can take its place. Love and forgiveness leads to alignment with the universe.

How does it work? I know they say love is mysterious but I am interested in the mechanics of this thing we call love and how to create more of it. We have already mentioned endlessly how when our vibration is raised, the energy of the universe begins to pour into our lives. But let's get more specific. This energy is pouring into our energy bodies or chakras. What chakra is associated with love? The heart chakra. So as this high vibrational energy enters into our crown chakra or vortex, it slowly makes its way down activating each chakra as it does. So it goes crown chakra, spiritual eye chakra, throat chakra, and then heart chakra. It is up for debate exactly how the chakras are activated and in which order, but I would suggest that it is not necessary to understand this. If we raise our personal vibration, it just happens. We will resonate better with these high vibrational energies of the universe and they will pour down into our vortex and chakras. Once the heart chakra is activated (or becomes engaged) we reach a critical mass which transforms our lives. Our hearts become a powerful engine sucking in ever greater quantities of this universal energy and clearing out all the other chakras. This is alignment with the infinite love of the universe. This is god.

Archons know this and are doing everything within their power to create a cycle of hatred in the world. They know that if they can foment fear and anger amongst peoples and nations that has the potential to create a vicious cycle which leads to wars in our world and a drastic lowering of our vibration. As Yoda said, "Fear leads to anger, anger leads to hate, hate leads to suffering."

Nationalistic wars are particularly insidious because they have the ability to reduce the vibration of entire nations. This is tragic but we need to understand that war is a buffet for the archons. They love it because it feeds their lust for low vibrational energy. An important thing to note about the archons is that they are very different from humans due to the fact that they have little to no creative ability. What they can do very well is influence the creations of others.

When it comes to wars, I don't think they have the ability even to start a war if they wanted to. What they can do is influence us to decide to create this reality for them. As we do this the vibration of the entire planet is lowered and they can operate more easily. I believe this is what is going on, kind of like a negative vortex. The more we give in to their agenda through our free will, the more they can take control. It is as if we are inviting them into our existence by our choices. At some point this negative vortex will lead to some sort of alignment with the matrix hive mind they are putting into place. Then it would be nearly impossible to overcome the world of the archons. Kind of like a black hole, once a threshold is passed there is no escape.

This is something we have a hard time understanding. These entities have no empathy and are working to create us in their image. They are hard-core Satanists and are driving this world to the brink of disaster. To them if a million civilians are killed in an unnecessary war, as was the case in Iraq, all the better. They get to feed off the low vibrational energy of death and destruction while simultaneously culling the population a bit. Up to this point they have kept us distracted by bread (hmm...) and circuses, but all that is about to change.

They know that the population of the planet is slowly waking up and seven billion conscious creators would be a tad difficult to manage. So I think in the years ahead, if the archons are not dealt with, we will see increased wars to further cull the population while simultaneously locking down those remaining into a matrix they can control. Their goal is not necessarily to eradicate all of humanity but rather to keep us at a number and vibrational state that is manageable. Kind of like cattle.

We have a chance to stop this but we need to take the steps now to break out of this low vibrational prism they are locking us into. We are like the giant in *Gulliver's Travels* that was tied down one tiny strand at a time until it was too late. Or a rotting corpse slowly being eaten away by maggots. It's time to wake the fuck up! There will come a threshold where it will be nearly impossible to resist the archon agenda but thankfully we are not there yet.

What we should be focused on now while there's still time is raising our individual vibrations and then we will have the strength and fortitude to wake others around us up. To do this we need unconditional love and forgiveness, get this, even for the archons. Yes, don't fall into the trap of hating them. That will only serve to make them stronger. What we need to do, no matter how difficult it may seem, is practice unconditional love for all creatures. This will sometimes take a sheer act of the will but it is our only hope. And as our alignment takes place and our heart chakra is engaged it will become like second nature to us.

This is probably the most difficult step to raising our vibration but also the most rewarding. Unconditional love means just that, there are no conditions for me to love you. It doesn't mean that we need to always be around low vibrational people. It does mean that we need to always have love and forgiveness in our hearts for the sake of our own vibration and alignment. While it is important to love and forgive others, it is equally important to love and forgive ourselves.

We really need to come to terms with this because unconditional love is the final firewall through which we must pass to attain full alignment, which means our vortex of creation is fully engaged and we are living our lives in a constant high vibrational state. We still have the ability to attain this alignment but it is not easy, and it is impossible if we have not done the vibrational foundation work to prepare for it.

So how do we do it? We don't. The only way to pass through this purification is by letting go. To simplify it, attachments cannot make this journey to full alignment, which is where we are headed once we start up this path of raising our vibration. As our vibration increases and our vortexes manifest faster and faster, we will be propelled towards reunification with our source. At that point it is sink or swim and we will need to make the decision to let go of all of our attachments in order to fully align with our source. I know this sounds scary, but it is just the unknown. We need to embrace it and become reconnected with the infinite consciousness of which we are a part.

If enough of us do this we can influence the vibration of our entire planet and this is the key that will unlock other important doors. As our collective vibration is raised, other high vibrational entities in our galaxy and universe will respond in ways we cannot even imagine at this point. But we need to make the choice and say no to the archons. Then they will need to leave due to the universal law of free will.

The choice is ours so let's begin by taking these very simple steps to raising our vibration. Everything else will happen automatically when we do and our lives will drastically improve. Thanks for reading.

"You have been activated."

Mission Impossible

Made in the USA
Lexington, KY
20 November 2018